Generative

A Revolution in Content Creation

Benjamin Evans

DEDICATION

To the relentless seekers of knowledge, the curious minds tirelessly decoding the mysteries of algorithms and code. This book is dedicated to you, the coders who embrace the challenges of neural networks with fervor and determination. May these pages serve as stepping stones on your journey, empowering you to unravel the complexities of this dynamic field and craft solutions that shape the future. Your passion fuels the innovation that drives our world forward, and for that, I extend my deepest gratitude and admiration.

CONTENTS

ACKNOWLEDGMENTS

I would like to extend my sincere gratitude to all those who have contributed to the realization of this book. First and foremost, I am indebted to my family for their unwavering support and encouragement throughout this endeavor. Their love and understanding have been my anchor in the stormy seas of writing.

I am deeply thankful to the experts whose guidance and insights have illuminated my path and enriched the content of this book. Their mentorship has been invaluable in shaping my understanding and refining my ideas.

I also extend my appreciation to those whose constructive feedback and insightful suggestions have helped polish this work to its finest form.

Furthermore, I am grateful to the countless individuals whose research, publications, and contributions have paved the way for the insights shared in these pages.

Last but not least, I express my heartfelt appreciation to the readers who embark on this journey with me. Your curiosity and engagement breathe life into these words, and it is for you that this book exists.

Thank you all for being part of this remarkable journey.

CHAPTER 1

Unveiling Generative AI

Imagine a world where artificial intelligence (AI) isn't just analyzing data, but creating entirely new things. This is the realm of generative AI, a revolutionary technology that's pushing the boundaries of what's possible. But what exactly is it, and how does it work? Let's embark on a journey to unveil the magic behind generative AI.

1.1 What is Generative AI?

Think of generative AI as a creative collaborator, an artist inspired by the vast amount of information it has access to. Unlike traditional AI that focuses on recognition or classification, generative AI takes a different approach. Instead of analyzing and categorizing existing data, it learns the underlying patterns and uses them to generate entirely new content. This content can be anything from text formats like poems or code, to visual creations like paintings or photorealistic images, and even music compositions.

Imagine you have a room full of children's drawings. Traditional AI might be able to identify the objects in the drawings, like flowers or houses. But generative AI, after studying those drawings, could create an entirely new children's drawing, complete with its own unique style and content.

1.2 Demystifying Generative Models

The key to generative AI's power lies in its use of generative models. These models are like sophisticated algorithms that are trained on massive datasets. As the model processes this data, it learns the intricate relationships and patterns within it. This allows the model to not only recognize existing patterns but also to predict and create entirely new ones.

Think of it like learning a new language. By immersing yourself in different conversations and reading texts, you begin to understand the grammar, vocabulary, and sentence structure. With enough exposure, you can then formulate your own sentences and even write a creative story. Generative models work similarly, but instead of words, they learn the underlying patterns of data, be it text, images, or even music.

1.3 A Historical Perspective: From Planning to Creation

The concept of AI creating new things isn't entirely new. Early AI research focused on creating "expert systems" that could solve problems or make decisions like a human expert. However, these systems relied on pre-programmed rules and knowledge. Generative AI represents a significant shift. It moves away from rigid rules and embraces the power of learning from data, allowing it to not just plan actions but to create entirely new possibilities.

Imagine the difference between a pre-written script for a play and a group of actors improvising a scene based on their characters and the overall theme. Traditional AI is like the script, following a set path. Generative AI, on the other hand, is like the improvisational actors, using their knowledge and creativity to generate something new and unexpected.

1.4 The Power of Unsupervised Learning

One of the key factors that enables generative AI to work its magic is a type of machine learning called unsupervised learning. Unlike supervised learning, where the AI is trained on data with labeled examples (like "cat" for a picture of a cat), unsupervised learning presents the AI with raw data and allows it to discover patterns on its own. This is like giving a child a box of blocks and letting them build whatever they imagine.

Imagine a vast library of books on various topics. Traditional, supervised learning would be like reading a book where each sentence is labeled with its grammatical function (noun, verb, etc.). Unsupervised learning, on the other hand, would be like simply reading the books and absorbing the overall language structure, themes, and vocabulary. This allows the AI to identify patterns and relationships that might not have been explicitly labeled.

This unsupervised learning approach allows generative AI to explore the vast possibilities within the data it's trained on. It's this exploration and discovery that empowers it to create truly novel and imaginative content.

CHAPTER 2

Unveiling the Magic: How Generative AI Works

We've lifted the veil on generative AI in Chapter 1, but how exactly does it turn raw data into captivating poems, breath-taking landscapes, or even symphonies?

2.1 Unveiling the Training Process: Data is King

Imagine a sculptor meticulously shaping a piece of clay. Generative AI works in a similar way, but instead of physical tools, it uses vast amounts of data to mold its creations. This data serves as the raw material, the foundation upon which the generative model learns and builds its creative prowess.

The quality and quantity of data are crucial. The more data a model is exposed to, the better it can understand the underlying patterns and relationships. For instance, a generative model trained on millions of images of cats will have a far superior grasp of feline features compared to one with only a handful.

The training process itself is like an iterative dance between the model and the data. The model analyzes the data, trying to capture the essence of what it's seeing. It then generates its own version, and this creation is compared back to the original data. Based on this comparison, the model refines its understanding and continues to generate new iterations, slowly getting closer to replicating the patterns and features within the data.

2.2 Exploring Different Architectures: From GANs to VAEs

Just like different artistic styles require different tools, generative AI utilizes various architectures to achieve its creative goals. Two prominent architectures include Generative Adversarial Networks (GANs) and Variational Autoencoders (VAEs).

- **Generative Adversarial Networks (GANs):** Imagine two teams, one creating art (the generator) and the other critiquing it (the discriminator). In a GAN, these two entities are constantly in competition. The generator strives to produce ever-more realistic creations, while the discriminator tries to differentiate between real data and the generator's output. This competitive dance pushes both sides to improve, ultimately leading to highly realistic and detailed outputs.

- **Variational Autoencoders (VAEs):** Picture a complex message compressed into a short code and then decoded back into its original form. VAEs work in a similar way. The model first compresses the data into a latent space, a lower-dimensional representation that captures the essence of the data. Then, it utilizes this latent space to generate new data points that share the same characteristics as the original data. VAEs are particularly adept at generating diverse and creative outputs while maintaining a consistent style.

These are just two examples of generative model architectures. Each has its strengths and weaknesses, and the choice of architecture depends on the specific task at hand. However, the underlying principle remains the same – using data to learn and then generate entirely new content.

2.3 Understanding Loss Functions: Shaping the Output

Imagine a sculptor constantly refining their work based on feedback. Generative models use a similar approach, employing a concept called a loss function. This function essentially measures the difference between the model's generated output and the desired outcome. The lower the loss, the closer the generated content is to the target.

By minimizing the loss function, the model learns to adjust its internal parameters, shaping its output to better match the characteristics of the training data. Think of it as the sculptor continuously chipping away at the clay, guided by their vision of the final masterpiece.

There are different types of loss functions, each tailored to specific goals. For instance, a loss function designed for generating realistic images might focus on pixel-level accuracy, while one for music generation might prioritize pitch and rhythm.

2.4 Evaluation Metrics: Measuring Success in Generation

Just like judging a painting at an art show, we need ways to evaluate the success of generative AI models. These evaluation metrics go beyond simply comparing the generated content to the original data. Here are some key factors considered:

- **Fidelity:** How closely does the generated content resemble the real data in terms of its characteristics and details?

- **Diversity:** Can the model generate a wide range of unique outputs, or is it repetitive?

- **Creativity:** Does the generated content go beyond simply mimicking the training data and showcase some level of originality?

- **Human Evaluation:** Ultimately, the human experience plays a role. Does the generated content feel natural, engaging, or even emotionally evocative?

By considering these metrics, we can gauge the effectiveness of generative models and identify areas for improvement. This continuous evaluation ensures that generative AI continues to evolve and produce increasingly impressive and groundbreaking creative outputs.

CHAPTER 3

A WORLD OF TEXT: GENERATIVE AI FOR LANGUAGE

The written word has always held immense power. It allows us to share ideas, weave stories, and connect across cultures. Now, generative AI is revolutionizing the realm of language, opening doors to new possibilities for creative expression and communication. Let's explore how generative AI is reshaping the world of text.

3.1 Text Generation: From Filling the Blanks to Crafting Stories

Imagine a world where writer's block becomes a relic of the past. Generative AI in text generation does just that. It can take a simple prompt, like a sentence fragment or a genre, and craft a complete and coherent piece of text.

This goes far beyond autocorrect or basic grammar

suggestions. Generative AI models can:

- **Fill in the Blanks:** Stuck on a sentence? Provide a starting point, and the model can generate creative continuations that fit the context and style.

- **Craft Compelling Content:** Need a catchy product description or an engaging blog post? Generative AI can churn out various options, saving you time and effort.

- **Dream Up Entire Stories:** Have a spark of an idea for a story? Generative AI can help you flesh it out, creating characters, dialogue, and plot twists, all while maintaining a consistent style and tone.

This technology isn't about replacing human writers, but rather about empowering them. It acts as a collaborator, brainstorming ideas and generating drafts that can be further refined and polished.

3. Automatic Writing Assistants: Boosting Creativity and Efficiency

Whether you're a novelist crafting a masterpiece or a student tackling an essay, generative AI can be your secret weapon. Automatic writing assistants leverage generative AI to streamline the writing process:

- **Overcome Writer's Block:** Stuck staring at a blank page? Generate prompts, outlines, or even initial paragraphs to kickstart your creativity.

- **Enhance Grammar and Style:** Worried about typos or unclear sentences? Generative AI can identify and suggest improvements, ensuring your writing is polished and professional.

- **Research and Fact-Checking:** Need to gather information or verify details? Generative AI can help you find relevant sources and ensure your writing is factually accurate.

These assistants become invaluable partners, streamlining the writing process and allowing you to focus on the bigger picture – expressing your ideas with clarity and impact.

3.3 Reimagine Translation: Breaking Down Language Barriers

Language barriers have long hindered communication and understanding. Generative AI is poised to revolutionize translation, making it faster, more accurate, and even more nuanced.

- **Breaking Down the Walls:** Generative AI models can translate languages with unprecedented fluency, capturing the essence and style of the original text.

- **Beyond Simple Word Substitution:** Generative AI understands the context and cultural nuances, ensuring the translated text conveys the intended meaning accurately.

- **Real-Time Communication:** Imagine seamless conversations happening across languages in real-time. Generative AI can facilitate this, fostering greater collaboration and understanding across borders.

This technology holds immense potential for fostering

global communication and connection.

3.4 Chatbots and Virtual Assistants: Powering Human-Machine Interaction

Generative AI isn't just about creating static text formats. It's also revolutionizing how we interact with machines through chatbots and virtual assistants.

- **Conversational AI:** Imagine having a natural conversation with a machine. Generative AI powers chatbots that understand context, respond in a human-like way, and can even adapt their responses based on the conversation flow.

- **Personalized Customer Service:** Generative AI chatbots can handle customer inquiries efficiently, providing personalized support and resolving issues effectively.

- **Always-Available Companions:** Virtual assistants powered by generative AI can become helpful companions, offering reminders, scheduling appointments, or simply engaging in stimulating conversation.

These applications showcase the potential of generative AI to bridge the gap between humans and machines, fostering a more intuitive and engaging interactive experience.

CHAPTER 4

BEYOND WORDS: GENERATIVE AI FOR IMAGES AND DESIGN

We've witnessed the power of generative AI in crafting captivating narratives and transforming written communication. But its potential stretches far beyond the realm of text.

4.1 Creating Art from Scratch: AI-Generated Masterpieces

Imagine a world where artistic expression transcends human limitations. Generative AI is pushing the boundaries of creativity, allowing us to generate stunning visuals from scratch.

- **AI-Powered Artists:** Simply provide a text description, like "a majestic castle floating in the clouds at sunset," and generative AI models can create a breathtakingly realistic image that captures your vision perfectly.

- **Dreamlike Landscapes and Surreal Compositions:** Have an idea for a fantastical world or a scene defying the laws of physics? Generative AI can bring your imagination to life, creating awe-inspiring visuals that blur the lines between reality and fantasy.

- **Exploring Artistic Styles:** Want to see your favorite photo reimagined in the style of Van Gogh or Picasso? Generative AI can seamlessly transform images, allowing you to explore the world through the lens of different artistic movements.

These AI-generated masterpieces aren't just visually stunning; they open doors for new artistic expressions and inspire a deeper appreciation for the creative process.

4.2 Photo Editing and Enhancement: Breathing New Life into Old Photos

Generative AI isn't just about creating new visuals; it's also transforming how we interact with existing ones. Here's how it's revolutionizing photo editing and enhancement:

- **Effortless Restoration:** Faded photographs or blurry images can be brought back to life. Generative AI can remove noise, sharpen details, and even colorize black and white photos, preserving precious memories for generations to come.

- **Creative Editing Tools:** Imagine adding elements to a photo that were never there – a majestic waterfall cascading down a mountainside, or a hot air balloon floating over a cityscape. Generative AI allows for seamless editing, adding a touch of magic to your photos.

- **Artistic Filters and Effects:** Want to give your photos a unique artistic flair? Generative AI filters can transform your images into paintings, sketches, or even classic film photographs, adding a touch of nostalgic charm.

Generative AI empowers anyone to become a photo editing pro, unlocking creative possibilities and allowing you to tell stories through your images in entirely new ways.

4.3 Revolutionizing Design: Prototyping and Product Development

The world of design is embracing generative AI to streamline the creation process and unlock innovative possibilities:

- **Rapid Prototyping:** Imagine generating multiple design variations for a product in a matter of seconds. Generative AI allows designers to explore different concepts quickly and efficiently, leading to more informed design decisions.

- **Personalized Design:** Catering to individual preferences is becoming easier. Generative AI can create custom product designs based on user input, leading to a more personalized and engaging user experience.

- **AI-Driven Material Exploration:** Developing new materials for products can be a time-consuming process. Generative AI can help by predicting material properties and suggesting innovative material combinations, accelerating the discovery of new possibilities.

Generative AI is becoming an essential tool for designers, fostering a faster, more creative, and data-driven design process.

4.4 Generative AI in Fashion: Designing for the Future

The fashion industry is also embracing the transformative power of generative AI:

- **AI-Generated Fashion Trends:** Predicting future fashion trends is no longer a guessing game. Generative AI can analyze vast amounts of data to identify emerging styles and patterns, allowing designers to stay ahead of the curve.

- **Personalized Clothing Design:** Imagine having a custom-designed outfit created just for you. Generative AI can take into account your body type, preferences, and even current fashion trends to create unique and flattering clothing designs.

- **Sustainable Design Practices:** The fashion industry has a significant environmental impact. Generative AI can help by optimizing fabric usage and suggesting more sustainable materials, leading to a more eco-conscious design approach.

Generative AI is poised to reshape the fashion industry, fostering a more personalized, sustainable, and future-focused approach to clothing design.

CHAPTER 5

A SYMPHONY OF CREATION: GENERATIVE AI FOR MUSIC AND AUDIO

The world of music has always held the power to evoke emotions, tell stories, and transport us to different worlds. Now, generative AI is adding a new dimension to this art form, composing melodies, crafting soundscapes, and revolutionizing the way we experience audio.

5.1 Composing Melodies and Creating Soundscapes

Imagine a world where anyone can become a composer. Generative AI is making this a reality, allowing users to create original music pieces from scratch.

- **AI-Powered Composition:** Simply provide a few musical elements, like a desired genre or a specific mood, and generative AI models can generate entire melodies, harmonies, and even orchestration.

- **Exploring Uncharted Sonic Territories:** Have a musical idea that defies traditional instruments or scales? Generative AI can create entirely new soundscapes, pushing the boundaries of musical expression and leading to the discovery of unique sonic palettes.

- **Collaboration Between Human and Machine:** Generative AI isn't meant to replace human musicians; it's here to collaborate. Musicians can use AI-generated elements as starting points or inspiration, sparking new creative directions in their music creation.

These capabilities are opening doors for both aspiring musicians and established artists, fostering a more inclusive and innovative musical landscape.

5.2 Music Personalization: Tailored Soundtracks for Every Mood

Music is a deeply personal experience. Generative AI is revolutionizing how we listen to music by personalizing it to our individual preferences and moods.

- **AI-Curated Playlists:** Imagine a playlist that perfectly reflects your current mood or activity. Generative AI can analyze your listening habits and create custom playlists that cater to your specific needs, whether it's a workout playlist or a soundtrack for relaxation.

- **Adaptive Music Scores:** Imagine movie scores that dynamically adapt to the on-screen action. Generative AI can create soundtracks that seamlessly change based on the emotions and tension levels of a scene, heightening the viewing experience.

- **Personalized Soundscapes for Different Environments:** Want to create a calming soundscape for your workspace or a lively atmosphere for a party? Generative AI can create custom soundscapes based on your desired environment, enhancing your everyday experiences.

This level of personalization allows us to engage with music in entirely new ways, making it an even more immersive and enriching part of our lives.

5.3 From Remixing to Restoration: Reimagining Audio Experiences

Generative AI isn't just about creating new audio experiences; it's also transforming how we interact with existing ones. Here's how it's impacting audio manipulation and restoration:

- **AI-Powered Remixing and Mashups:** Imagine seamlessly blending different songs or genres to create unique remixes. Generative AI can analyze the musical structure and elements of different tracks, allowing for creative remixes that maintain the original feel while adding a fresh twist.

- **Historical Audio Restoration:** Faded recordings or damaged audio can be brought back to life. Generative AI can remove noise, imperfections, and even enhance sound quality, preserving precious audio recordings for future generations.

- **Automatic Content Creation for Video and Games:** Creating sound effects and background music for video content can be time-consuming. Generative AI can automate this process, generating appropriate audio elements based on the visual content, making content creation more efficient.

This technology unlocks creative possibilities for both professional audio producers and casual users alike, allowing for the manipulation and restoration of audio in entirely new ways.

5.4 The Future of Sound Design: AI-Powered Audio Production

The world of audio production is embracing generative AI

as a valuable tool:

- **Streamlining Sound Design Workflows:** Creating complex sound effects or audio samples for films and games can be a tedious process. Generative AI can automate repetitive tasks and suggest creative sound design elements, accelerating the audio production process.

- **AI-Assisted Sound Design Exploration:** Imagine exploring a vast library of sound effects and finding the perfect one for your project. Generative AI can suggest sound options based on your desired mood and sonic characteristics, saving time and effort during the sound design process.

- **Personalized Audio Branding:** Creating a unique sonic identity for a brand is crucial. Generative AI can help by analyzing competitor soundscapes and suggesting unique audio elements that reflect the brand's personality.

By streamlining workflows, fueling exploration, and

assisting in creative decision-making, generative AI is becoming an essential tool for sound designers, shaping the future of audio production.

CHAPTER 6

SHAPING THE FUTURE: GENERATIVE AI IN SCIENCE AND ENGINEERING

Generative AI isn't just about creating captivating art or personalized experiences; it's poised to revolutionize the fields of science and engineering. Imagine a world where AI helps us design life-saving drugs, predict climate change with unprecedented accuracy, and optimize engineering processes – that's the exciting future generative AI promises.

6.1 Drug Discovery and Material Science: Accelerating Scientific Progress

The journey from scientific discovery to a new drug or material can be long and arduous. Generative AI is accelerating this process in fascinating ways:

- **Designing New Drugs:** Imagine AI sifting through vast databases of molecules and chemical structures to identify potential candidates for new drugs. Generative AI models can predict the properties of new compounds, saving years of traditional laboratory testing and accelerating the development of life-saving treatments.

- **Optimizing Material Properties:** Creating new materials with specific properties for engineering applications is often a trial-and-error process. Generative AI can analyze existing materials and suggest novel material combinations with desired properties, leading to the discovery of groundbreaking materials for various uses.

By analyzing vast amounts of data and identifying patterns that might escape human researchers, generative AI is becoming an invaluable tool for scientific discovery and material science innovation.

6.2 Climate Change Modeling: Generating Realistic Simulations

Climate change is one of the most pressing challenges facing humanity. Generative AI offers a powerful tool for understanding and predicting its impact:

- **Creating Realistic Climate Models:** Imagine AI models simulating the complex interactions between the atmosphere, oceans, and land. Generative AI can create highly realistic climate models, allowing scientists to predict future climate scenarios with greater accuracy, informing crucial decision-making.

- **Generating Data for Climate Research:** Collecting climate data can be expensive and time-consuming. Generative AI can supplement existing data by creating realistic simulations of past and future climate conditions, giving scientists a more comprehensive understanding of our changing planet.

By enabling researchers to test different scenarios and

better understand climate change dynamics, generative AI plays a crucial role in combating this global challenge.

6.3 Generative AI in Engineering: Optimizing Designs and Processes

The world of engineering is embracing generative AI to optimize designs, improve efficiency, and unlock new possibilities:

- **AI-Powered Design Optimization:** Imagine designing a bridge that can withstand earthquakes or an airplane wing with superior aerodynamic performance. Generative AI can analyze countless design iterations and suggest optimized solutions that meet specific engineering requirements.

- **Streamlining Manufacturing Processes:** Manufacturing processes can be complex and prone to inefficiencies. Generative AI can analyze production data and suggest optimizations for workflow, resource allocation, and even predictive maintenance, leading to a smoother and more efficient manufacturing process.

From optimizing bridge designs to streamlining assembly lines, generative AI is becoming an essential tool for engineers, leading to more efficient, innovative, and robust engineering solutions.

6.4 The Ethics of AI-Generated Data: Ensuring Transparency and Fairness

The power of generative AI comes with a responsibility to ensure its ethical use. Here's how we can ensure transparency and fairness in AI-generated data:

- **Understanding the Biases:** Generative AI models are trained on existing data, which may contain inherent biases. It's crucial to identify and address these biases to ensure that the generated data is fair and representative.

- **Transparency in Model Development:**

Understanding how generative models work and the data they are trained on is critical. Transparency allows for ethical oversight and ensures that AI-generated data isn't misused.

- **Human Oversight and Collaboration:** While generative AI is powerful, human oversight and collaboration remain essential. Scientists and engineers can guide the development and application of generative AI, ensuring it serves humanity's best interests.

By addressing these ethical considerations, we can ensure that generative AI remains a force for good, driving scientific progress and fostering a more sustainable future.

CHAPTER 7

GENERATIVE AI FOR THE MASSES: USER-FRIENDLY TOOLS AND APPLICATIONS

Generative AI isn't just for tech giants and research labs anymore. This chapter dives into the exciting world of user-friendly tools and applications, making generative AI accessible to everyone. Get ready to unleash your inner creator and experience the power of AI-powered personalization.

7.1 Democratizing Creativity: Accessible Generative AI Platforms

Imagine a world where anyone, regardless of technical expertise, can create stunning visuals, captivating music, or even compelling stories. Well, that world is here. User-friendly generative AI platforms are making this powerful technology accessible to the masses.

- **Intuitive Interfaces:** Gone are the days of complex coding or data manipulation. User-friendly platforms present clear interfaces with simple controls, allowing anyone to experiment with generative AI features.

- **Pre-Trained Models and Templates:** Don't start from scratch! These platforms offer pre-trained generative models and templates that cater to a variety of creative needs, making it easy to jump right in and start creating.

- **Community and Collaboration:** User-friendly platforms often foster vibrant online communities where users can share their creations, get feedback, and learn from each other, accelerating the creative journey.

These user-friendly platforms empower everyone to become a creator, democratizing the realm of artistic expression and fostering a new wave of creative innovation.

7.2 The Rise of AI-Powered Content Creation Tools

Content creation, be it for marketing, education, or even personal expression, can be a time-consuming task. However, AI-powered content creation tools are revolutionizing the process:

- **AI-Generated Design Assets:** Need a catchy banner for your website or a unique social media post? These tools can generate graphics, logos, and other visual elements based on your input, saving you time and effort.

- **AI-Powered Writing Assistants:** Stuck staring at a blank page? Don't worry! AI writing assistants can help by generating content outlines, suggesting creative writing prompts, and even polishing your grammar and style.

- **AI-Driven Music Composition:** Unleash your inner musician! These tools can generate melodies, harmonies, and even background music based on your desired genre or mood, allowing you to create custom soundtracks with ease.

These AI-powered tools act as your creative collaborators, streamlining the content creation process and allowing you to focus on your unique vision and message.

7.3 Personalization at Scale: Customizing Experiences with Generative AI

Personalization is no longer a luxury; it's an expectation. Generative AI is making it possible to tailor experiences to individual preferences at an unprecedented scale:

- **AI-Curated Recommendations:** Imagine a news feed that anticipates your interests or a shopping platform that suggests products you'll actually love. Generative AI can analyze your past behavior and preferences to recommend content and products that resonate with you.

- **Adaptive Learning Experiences:** Learning should be tailored to individual needs. Generative AI can create personalized learning materials and adjust the difficulty level based on a student's progress, leading to a more engaging and effective learning experience.

- **Customizable Entertainment:** Imagine a movie that adapts to your mood or a video game that adjusts its difficulty based on your skill level. Generative AI can personalize entertainment experiences, making them more engaging and immersive.

By tailoring content and experiences to individual preferences, generative AI is changing the way we interact with the digital world, making it feel more relevant and engaging.

7.4 The Future of Work: AI as a Collaborative Partner

The future of work is one of collaboration, not competition, between humans and AI. Generative AI is poised to become a valuable partner in various work environments:

- **Brainstorming and Creative Exploration:** Stuck trying to solve a problem or develop a new idea? Generative AI can suggest innovative solutions or spark creative ideas, leading to more efficient brainstorming sessions.

- **Automating Repetitive Tasks:** Many jobs involve repetitive tasks that can be automated. Generative AI can handle these tasks, freeing up human workers to focus on more strategic and creative endeavors.

- **Enhanced Data Analysis and Decision-Making:** Businesses generate vast amounts of data. Generative AI can analyze this data and identify patterns that humans might miss, leading to more informed decision-making.

Generative AI isn't here to replace human workers; rather, it's here to augment our capabilities, allowing us to work smarter and focus on tasks that require human judgment, creativity, and social skills.

CHAPTER 8

THE ART OF THE PROMPT: MASTERING GENERATIVE AI INPUTS

Imagine you're an orchestra conductor, leading a group of talented musicians. Just like the conductor sets the tone and direction for the music, the prompt you provide is your way of guiding generative AI.

8.1 Crafting Effective Prompts: Guiding the AI in the Right Direction

The prompt is the foundation of your interaction with generative AI. It's the starting point that tells the model what you want it to create. Here's how to craft effective prompts:

- **Clarity and Specificity:** The more specific your prompt, the better the AI can understand your vision. Instead of saying "paint a landscape," try "paint a vibrant desert landscape at sunset with a lone cactus silhouetted against the sky."

- **Provide Context and Details:** Don't be afraid to add details! Specify the desired style (realistic, impressionistic), mood (peaceful, dramatic), or even color palette to guide the AI towards your desired outcome.

- **Reference Images and Examples:** Visual inspiration can be incredibly helpful. Include links to images or describe existing works of art that capture the style or mood you're aiming for.

By crafting clear, specific, and detailed prompts, you provide the AI with a roadmap to generate outputs that align with your vision.

8.2 Understanding Prompt Engineering: Unlocking the Full Potential

Crafting effective prompts is more than just providing basic instructions. Prompt engineering is an art form that helps you leverage the full potential of generative AI:

- **Experiment with Different Wording:** Sometimes, subtle changes in phrasing can drastically alter the output. Try rephrasing your prompt and see how the AI responds.

- **Utilize Keywords and Phrases:** Certain keywords can trigger specific styles or effects within the AI model. Research popular keywords and experiment with incorporating them into your prompts.

- **Leverage Advanced Techniques:** As you become more comfortable, explore advanced prompt engineering techniques like negation (specifying what you don't want) or combining different styles and elements within a single prompt.

By understanding prompt engineering, you become more than just a user; you become a collaborator, influencing and shaping the creative direction of the AI.

8.3 Leveraging Human-AI Collaboration: The Best of

Both Worlds

Generative AI isn't meant to replace human creativity; it's here to augment it. The most successful applications leverage human-AI collaboration:

- **Humans Set the Vision, AI Executes:** Use your creativity and imagination to come up with a concept or idea. Then, let the AI generate different variations or interpretations, allowing you to explore various possibilities.

- **Refine and Iterate:** The first output might not be perfect. Use your human judgment to refine the prompt, providing feedback to the AI and guiding it closer to your desired outcome.

- **Human Creativity Meets AI Efficiency:** Let the AI handle the repetitive tasks of generating variations or exploring different styles. This frees you up to focus on the higher-level creative decisions and adding your unique human touch.

By embracing human-AI collaboration, you create a powerful synergy that unleashes the full potential of both creative forces.

8.4 Exploring Creative Exploration Techniques: Pushing the Boundaries

Don't be afraid to experiment and push the boundaries of what's possible with generative AI. Here are some techniques to spark your creative exploration:

- **Start with Random Prompts:** Sometimes, unexpected results can lead to groundbreaking ideas. Generate random prompts and see what the AI comes up with. It might spark a new creative direction you hadn't considered.

- **Combine Different Styles:** Imagine a world where a Van Gogh landscape meets a classic Japanese woodblock print. Experiment with combining different artistic styles or genres within your prompts.

- **Challenge the AI:** Don't be afraid to give the AI seemingly impossible tasks. Prompt it to create nonsensical objects or impossible landscapes – you might be surprised by the creative results.

By embracing exploration and experimentation, you unlock the true power of generative AI as a tool for creative discovery and pushing the boundaries of artistic expression.

CHAPTER 9

NAVIGATING THE ETHICAL LANDSCAPE: RESPONSIBLE DEVELOPMENT AND USE

Generative AI holds immense potential to revolutionize various aspects of our lives. However, with such power comes responsibility.

9.1 Bias and Fairness in Generative AI: Mitigating Algorithmic Discrimination

Generative AI models are trained on vast datasets. If these datasets contain inherent biases, the AI will perpetuate those biases in its outputs. Here's how we can ensure fairness:

- **Identifying and Mitigating Bias in Training Data:** We must scrutinize the data used to train generative AI models and identify potential biases. Techniques like data augmentation and bias correction algorithms can help mitigate these biases.

- **Promoting Diversity and Inclusion in Development Teams:** The people creating and developing generative AI models should represent diverse perspectives. This diversity ensures that the technology reflects a broader range of viewpoints and minimizes the risk of bias.

- **Transparency and Explainability:** Understanding how generative AI models arrive at their outputs is crucial. Transparency allows developers and users to identify and address potential biases within the system.

By actively addressing bias in training data, development teams, and the models themselves, we can ensure that generative AI promotes fairness and inclusivity.

9.2 Ownership and Copyright: Who Owns AI-Generated Content?

As generative AI creates original content, questions arise about ownership and copyright. Here's how we can navigate this uncharted territory:

- **Distinguishing Between User Input and AI Contribution:** The level of human input should be a factor in determining ownership. If a human provides a detailed prompt and refines the output, they might hold more ownership than someone using a simple prompt.

- **Clear Licensing Models for AI-Generated Content:** Developing clear licensing models specifying ownership and usage rights is crucial. This will provide creators and users with a framework for utilizing AI-generated content responsibly.

- **Open Collaboration and Shared Ownership:** In some cases, collaborative models where both humans and AI share ownership of the generated content might be appropriate. This could encourage innovation and fairly distribute the benefits of AI-generated creativity.

Open discussions and legal frameworks are necessary to establish clear ownership rights and ensure fair treatment of creators and users of AI-generated content.

9.3 Deepfakes and Misinformation: Combating the Spread of AI-Generated Lies

Generative AI can be misused to create deepfakes, realistic videos or audio recordings that manipulate reality. This poses a significant threat to the spread of misinformation. Here's how we can combat this:

- **Developing Deepfake Detection Tools:** Technology companies and researchers are developing tools to identify and flag deepfakes. These tools will help users discern genuine content from manipulated media.

- **Promoting Media Literacy:** Educating the public

on how to critically evaluate online content is crucial. By understanding the potential for manipulation, users can be more discerning of the information they encounter.

- **Promoting Transparency and Accountability:** Holding those who create and spread deepfakes accountable is essential. Clear regulations and consequences can deter malicious actors from using AI for harmful purposes.

By working together, technology companies, governments, and the public can mitigate the threat of deepfakes and ensure responsible use of generative AI.

9.4 The Future of Regulation: Shaping AI Development for Good

Generative AI is a rapidly evolving field. Developing responsible regulations is crucial:

- **Focus on Ethical Principles:** Regulations should be

built upon ethical principles such as fairness, transparency, and accountability. These principles should guide the development and use of generative AI.

- **International Collaboration:** The potential impact of AI is global. International collaboration on regulatory frameworks can ensure consistent and ethical development across borders.

- **Balancing Innovation and Public Safety:** Regulations should strike a balance between encouraging innovation and protecting the public from potential harms. This requires ongoing dialogue between policymakers, technologists, and the public.

By establishing clear, ethical, and adaptable regulations, we can ensure that generative AI continues to flourish and contribute positively to society.

CHAPTER 10

THE GENERATIVE AI HORIZON: A GLIMPSE INTO THE FUTURE

Generative AI is no longer science fiction; it's rapidly becoming a reality woven into the fabric of our lives. As we peer into the future, a world brimming with creative possibilities and groundbreaking applications awaits.

10.1 The Symbiosis of Human and Machine Creativity

Imagine a future where human and machine creativity exist in a state of beautiful symbiosis. Generative AI won't replace artists, writers, or musicians; it will become their powerful collaborator:

- **Breaking Through Creative Blocks:** Stuck on a project? AI can suggest unexpected ideas, spark new creative directions, and help overcome creative hurdles.

- **Amplifying Human Imagination:** The human mind is a wellspring of creativity. Generative AI can act as an amplifier, taking initial ideas and generating countless variations, allowing humans to explore a wider creative landscape.

- **Democratizing Artistic Expression:** Generative AI tools will become even more user-friendly, empowering everyone to tap into their creative potential and express themselves in new ways.

This future collaboration between humans and AI promises a new era of artistic expression, pushing the boundaries of what's possible and enriching our cultural landscape.

10.2 Generative AI in Education: Personalized Learning Experiences

Education is on the cusp of a transformative era. Generative AI holds immense potential to personalize the learning experience for every student:

- **Adaptive Learning Systems:** Imagine AI-powered platforms that tailor learning materials and difficulty levels to each student's individual needs and pace. This personalized approach can lead to a more engaging and effective learning experience for all.

- **AI-Powered Tutors and Virtual Assistants:** Generative AI can create intelligent tutors that provide personalized feedback, answer questions, and offer additional learning resources, enhancing the student-teacher dynamic.

- **Immersive Learning Environments:** Generative AI can create immersive learning experiences, allowing students to explore historical events, travel to different parts of the world virtually, or experiment with complex concepts in a safe and interactive environment.

By personalizing learning, AI can unlock the full potential of every student, fostering a love for learning and preparing them for a future filled with possibilities.

10.3 The Future of Entertainment: AI-Powered Storytelling and Games

The world of entertainment is on the verge of a revolution. Generative AI promises to transform the way we experience stories and games:

- **Interactive Storytelling:** Imagine stories that adapt to your choices, characters that evolve based on your interactions, and narratives that unfold in a truly interactive way. Generative AI can create these dynamic and personalized storytelling experiences.

- **AI-Generated Game Worlds:** Generative AI can craft vast and ever-evolving game worlds with endless possibilities. Imagine exploring procedurally generated landscapes, encountering unique characters, and embarking on unpredictable adventures.

- **Personalized Entertainment Experiences:** AI can recommend movies, music, or games that align perfectly with your preferences. Get ready for a future of entertainment experiences curated just for you.

Generative AI is poised to redefine entertainment, blurring the lines between passive consumption and active participation, and creating a new era of immersive and engaging experiences.

10.4 A New Era of Innovation: Generative AI Driving Progress Across Industries

The impact of generative AI will extend far beyond entertainment and education. It's poised to usher in a new era of innovation across various industries:

- **Scientific Discovery:** AI can analyze vast datasets and identify patterns that might escape human researchers, accelerating breakthroughs in medicine, materials science, and other scientific fields.

- **Engineering and Design:** Generative AI can optimize designs, streamline manufacturing processes, and even suggest innovative solutions to complex engineering challenges.

- **Personalized Products and Services:** Imagine custom-designed clothes that perfectly fit your body or financial products tailored to your unique needs. Generative AI can make personalized experiences a reality across various sectors.

From accelerating scientific discovery to revolutionizing product design, generative AI has the potential to unlock a new era of progress across various industries, shaping a better future for all.

As we conclude our exploration of generative AI, let's remember that the future is bright. This powerful technology holds immense potential to enhance our creativity, personalize our experiences, and drive innovation across all aspects of our lives. By embracing generative AI responsibly and ethically, we can unlock a future filled with wonder, possibility, and progress.

ABOUT THE AUTHOR

Writer's Bio:

 Benjamin Evans, a respected figure in the tech world, is known for his insightful commentary and analysis. With a strong educational background likely in fields such as computer science, engineering, or business, he brings a depth of knowledge to his discussions on emerging technologies and industry trends. Evans' knack for simplifying complex concepts, coupled with his innate curiosity and passion for innovation, has established him as a go-to source for understanding the dynamics of the digital landscape. Through articles, speeches, and social media, he shares his expertise and offers valuable insights into the impact of technology on society.